Tigers and Lions

François Bissonnette

ISBN 10: 1542914809
ISBN-13: 978-1542914802

Animal Books for Children Collection

Tigers

Hello!

My name is Sinbad, and I am a tiger.

I belong to the *Felidae* family.

I belong to the same family as lions, leopards and little house cats.

We, tigers, are the biggest of all the cat species. We have reddish-orange fur with vertical dark stripes.

A full grown male tiger can reach a total length of up to 3.3 meters (11 feet) and weigh 300 kilograms (660 pounds).

We live in Asia, particularly in Indonesia, Malaysia, Thailand, Russia, Vietnam, southern China, Cambodia, Laos and Myanmar.

There's only about 3,000 to 4,500 tigers that remain in the wild.

I know, it's really sad. We are in danger of extinction.

There are only 6 out of 9 subspecies of tigers alive today.

The 6 subspecies of tigers still alive are, the Bengal tiger, the Siberian tiger, the Sumatran tiger, the Malayan tiger, the Indochinese tiger, and the South China tiger.

The 3 extinct subspecies are the Caspian tiger, the Bali tiger and the Javan tiger.

White tigers, like me, are not a subspecies. We are Bengal tigers that possess a specific gene that gives us our white fur.

Did you know that the tiger's tongue, like all cat's tongue, is rough because it is covered with papillae? Papillae are tiny backward-facing barbs.

Like little cats, we use our tongue to clean and comb our fur.

Unlike most of the other cats, we, tigers, are really good swimmers and often cool off in lakes during hot days.

Naturally, tigers also drink water.

We are carnivores. We eat animals such as wild pigs, moose, deer, cows, goats and buffalos.

Unlike lions, we are mostly solitary animals and we generally hunt at night. Our night vision is about six times better than humans'.

We can run at a speed of 65 km/h (40 mph) over short distances.

Did you know that each tiger's stripes pattern is unique?

We have 30 teeth in our mouths that are extremely sharp.

Our upper canines can be as long as 7 cm (3 inches).

Little tigers cubs, like me, stay with their mother until they reach 24 to 30 months of age.

We are big sleepers. Tigers sleep around 16 to 20 hours a day.

We can live 15 years in the wild and 20 to 25 years in captivity. I really love being a tiger.

Lions

Hello! My name is Charles, and I am a lion.

I belong to the *Felidae* family.

I belong to the same family as tigers, leopards and little house cats.

We, lions, are the second biggest cat after the tigers. We are called King of the Jungle, but in reality we live in the open savannas of Africa.

There are no more than 30,000 to 100,000 lions that remain in all of Africa.

There are also about 350 Asiatic lions that live in India's Gir Forest.

Like tigers we are in danger of extinction.

We have yellow-brown fur and male lions are the only cats who have a mane.

A full grown male lion can reach a total length of up to 2.7 meters (8.85 feet) and weigh 220 kilograms (485 pounds).

Unlike tigers and other cats we are very social animals. We live in groups of 10 to 30 lions. These groups are called prides.

We are very affectionate towards each other: rubbing heads and grooming.

We work together to defend our territory.

Female lions do almost all of the hunting while the males protect the pride.

Like tigers our night vision is about six times better than humans' and we have more success when we hunt at night.

We are carnivores and we hunt, among others, antelopes, buffaloes, zebras, wild hogs, giraffes and even crocodiles and snakes.

If available, we also drink water every day.

Lionesses are caring mothers and the cubs are extremely playful.

Did you know that the roar of a lion can be heard 8 kilometers (5 miles) away?

Like other cats we use our tongue to clean and comb our fur.

We usually sleep 16 to 20 hours per day.

We, lions, are pretty fast runner. We can run at a speed of 80 km/h (50 mph) over short distances.

We can live about 12 years in the wild and 25 years in captivity. I love being a lion.

From the same collection

Elephants and Giraffes

François Bissonnette

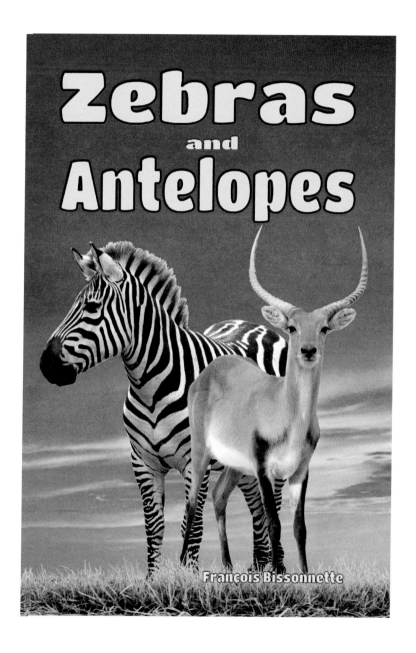

Made in the USA
Middletown, DE
28 January 2022